France

KAITE GOLDSWORTHY

MEDIA ENHANCED BOOKS
AV2 BY WEIGL™
ADDED VALUE • AUDIO VISUAL

www.av2books.com

MEDIA ENHANCED BOOKS
AV²
BY WEIGL™
ADDED VALUE • AUDIO VISUAL

AV² provides enriched content that supplements and complements this book. Weigl's AV² books strive to create inspired learning and engage young minds in a total learning experience.

Your AV² Media Enhanced books come alive with...

Audio
Listen to sections of the book read aloud.

Key Words
Study vocabulary, and complete a matching word activity.

Video
Watch informative video clips.

Quizzes
Test your knowledge.

Embedded Weblinks
Gain additional information for research.

Slide Show
View images and captions, and prepare a presentation.

Try This!
Complete activities and hands-on experiments.

... and much, much more!

Go to **www.av2books.com**, and enter this book's unique code.

BOOK CODE

X 4 8 8 5 8 9

AV² by Weigl brings you media enhanced books that support active learning.

Published by AV² by Weigl
350 5th Avenue, 59th Floor
New York, NY 10118
Websites: www.av2books.com   www.weigl.com

Library of Congress Cataloging-in-Publication Data

Goldsworthy, Kaite.
 France / Kaite Goldsworthy.
    pages cm. — (Exploring countries)
Includes index.
 ISBN 978-1-4896-1010-2 (hardcover : alk. paper) — ISBN 978-1-4896-1011-9 (softcover : alk. paper) —
ISBN 978-1-4896-1012-6 (single user ebk.) — ISBN 978-1-4896-1013-3 (multi user ebk.)
1. France—Juvenile literature. I. Title.
DC17.G65 2014
 944—dc23   2014005941

Printed in the United States of America in North Mankato, Minnesota
1 2 3 4 5 6 7 8 9 0   18 17 16 15 14

042014
WEP150314

Project Coordinator Heather Kissock
Art Director Terry Paulhus

Photo Credits
Every reasonable effort has been made to trace ownership and to obtain permission to reprint copyright material. The publishers would be pleased to have any errors or omissions brought to their attention so that they may be corrected in subsequent printings.

Weigl acknowledges Getty Images as its primary image supplier for this title.

Contents

France Overview

France, located on the continent of Europe, is known around the world for its history, art, and culture. The scenic country has mountain ranges, fertile farmland, rivers, forests, and coastlines with beautiful sandy beaches. The French **economy** is the ninth-largest in the world, and many residents of France enjoy a high quality of life. France is one of Europe's oldest nations. It is an original member of the European Union (EU), an economic and political organization with 28 countries. Mainland France and the island of Corsica, in the Mediterranean Sea, are called metropolitan France. France, officially named the French Republic, also has territories in South America, the Caribbean, and the South Pacific.

Chambord is a 500-year-old château, or castle, in the Loire Valley.

Farmers grow fields of sunflowers in the south of France. France produces more sunflowers than any other country in the EU.

On July 14th, the French celebrate their national holiday, Bastille Day, with parades and fireworks. On that date in 1789, a mob attacked a prison called the Bastille, starting the French Revolution.

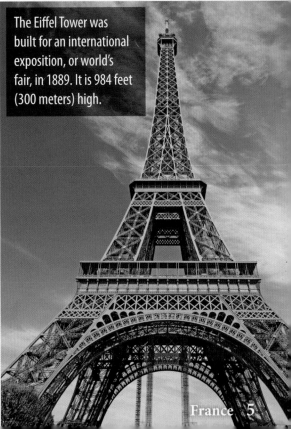

The Eiffel Tower was built for an international exposition, or world's fair, in 1889. It is 984 feet (300 meters) high.

People in France enjoy sitting at outdoor cafés for a meal or something to drink.

Exploring France

In terms of area, France is the largest country in Western Europe. It extends 598 miles (962 kilometers) from north to south. From east to west, it spans 590 miles (950 km). People often call France "the hexagon" because its shape is roughly six-sided. France borders the countries of Belgium, Luxembourg, Germany, Switzerland, Italy, Monaco, Spain, and Andorra. It also touches several major bodies of water. They are the North Sea and the English Channel to the north, the Bay of Biscay and the Atlantic Ocean to the west, and the Mediterranean Sea to the south.

N

Spain

Loire River

Map Legend

France

Land

Water

Loire River

▲ Mont Blanc

Côte d'Azur

📍 Capital City

SCALE ▬▬▬▬ 500 Miles

500 Kilometers

Loire River

The Loire is France's longest river. It extends 634 miles (1,020 km) from the southeast through central and western France. The Loire reaches the Atlantic Ocean near the port of Saint-Nazaire.

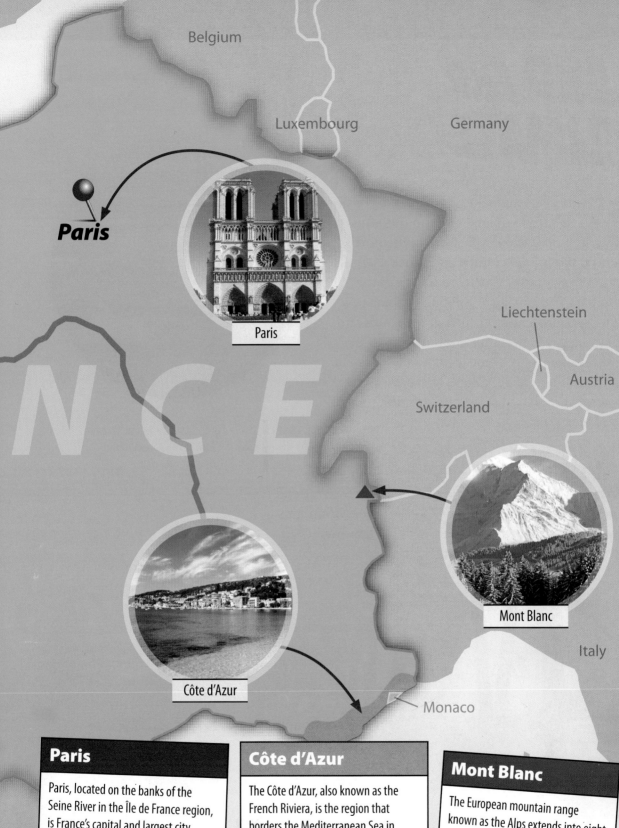

Belgium

Luxembourg

Germany

Liechtenstein

Austria

Switzerland

Italy

Paris

Paris

Côte d'Azur

Mont Blanc

Monaco

Paris

Paris, located on the banks of the Seine River in the Île de France region, is France's capital and largest city. Paris has many cultural and historic attractions. It is often called the City of Light because many buildings and monuments are lit up at night.

Côte d'Azur

The Côte d'Azur, also known as the French Riviera, is the region that borders the Mediterranean Sea in southeastern France. *Côte d'azur* means "azure coast" in French. Azure is the color of the sea's light blue water in this popular resort area.

Mont Blanc

The European mountain range known as the Alps extends into eight countries, including France. The highest peak in Western Europe is Mont Blanc in the French Alps. It is 15,771 feet (4,807 m) high.

LAND AND CLIMATE

France has many lowland areas, or basins, and several upland and mountainous regions. The Paris Basin, in the north-central part of the country, is France's largest natural region. It covers one-fourth of the country. The smaller Aquitaine Basin is in southwestern France. Much of the south and east is rugged and mountainous. However, these regions have some lowland plains, such as the Rhône-Saône Valley. There are large swampy areas in the Camargue region, near the Mediterranean.

France has five main mountain ranges. The oldest is the **Massif** Central in south-central France. The French Alps stretch along the border with Switzerland and Italy. The Jura Mountains and Vosges Mountains are north of the Alps in the east. In the southwest, the Pyrenees separate France and Spain.

Located in the Massif Central, Volcano Regional Park in Auverge has four chains of extinct volcanoes.

Besides the Loire, France's major rivers include the Rhône, Seine, and Garonne. The Rhône, which begins in the Alps and flows through the Massif Central, is the deepest. The Saône River, which begins in the Vosges Mountains, is a major **tributary** of the Rhône. The Seine starts in eastern France and flows northwest to the English Channel. The Garonne flows from the Pyrenees through southwestern France to the Atlantic. Many of France's rivers are connected by canals.

The climate varies across France. Northern and western France have an oceanic climate. Mild, damp weather is blown in by winds traveling from west to east over the Atlantic Ocean, making summers cooler and winters milder. Northeastern France has colder, snowier winters and hotter summers. In the south, near the Mediterranean, summers are hot and dry, and winters are very mild. The coldest climates in France are found in the Alps and Pyrenees. There, snowfall is common during the winter, and there are **glaciers** year-round.

With nearly 4,200 miles (6,700 km) of rivers and canals, France has the largest waterway network in Europe. Most of the country can be reached by boat.

45 MILES PER HOUR
Average speed of the mistral, a cold northerly wind that blows at times toward France's Mediterranean coast. (72 km per hour)

2,130 Miles Length of the coastline of France. (3,428 km)

248,573
Total area of France in square miles. (643,801 sq. km)

$\frac{2}{3}$ Fraction of France's landscape that is plains.

PLANTS AND ANIMALS

136 Number of tree species in France.

More than 4,500 plant **species** and 750 animal species live in France. The warm southern part of the country is home to fruit and olive trees, vines, and herbs. The Provence region is known for wildflowers and lavender. Oak, chestnut, and beech trees are plentiful in central and northern France. Birch, poplar, and willow also grow there. Juniper, pine, fir, and spruce trees are more common in the **alpine** areas of the country. France has many old trees, including Le Chêne Chapelle, or the Chapel Oak. This tree is about 800 years old.

Numerous animals in France are also common in other Western European countries. Several types of deer, such as the roe deer and red deer, live in France. Wild boars, or sangliers, are common in the countryside. Foxes, badgers, beavers, and otters live in many areas of France. Herds of wild horses live in the Camargue. The Alps and Pyrenees are home to brown bears, wolves, lynx, and alpine marmots.

30 Miles Per Hour Speed a wild boar can run. (48 km per hour)

30% Portion of France that is forest.

42,000 Number of plane trees that line the Canal du Midi, Europe's oldest functioning canal.

7% Portion of France covered by nature parks.

Wild boars can be quite large, sometimes weighing as much as 660 pounds (300 kilograms).

NATURAL RESOURCES

One of France's most important natural resources is its rich soil. Most of the country is covered in brown earth soil, in which many types of crops grow well. Some crops thrive in the Mediterranean soil found in the south of France. The country's soils and climate help make France one of the largest sources of agricultural products in the European Union.

Almost two-thirds of France's crops are grains, including wheat, barley, oats, and corn. Sunflowers and rapeseed are grown mainly for the cooking oil made from their seeds. French farmers are the third-largest vegetable producers in the EU. France's largest fruit crop is apples.

France is not rich in mineral and energy resources. Some iron, coal, oil, and natural gas are mined. Small quantities of uranium are produced in the Massif Central, **potash** in the Alsace region, and sulfur in the Aquitaine Basin.

France uses its rivers as a source of energy. About 8 percent of the country's electricity is produced using **hydropower**. However, nuclear power plants are the most important source of electricity.

Natural Resources BY THE NUMBERS

5th France's rank among the world's largest wheat-producing countries.

20% Portion of agricultural goods in the EU produced by France.

1906 Year that an explosion at the Courrières mine in northern France killed more than 1,000 people, making it Europe's worst mining disaster.

490,000 Approximate number of farms in France.

75% Portion of the electricity used in France that comes from nuclear power plants.

Vineyards grow grapes of many varieties in all regions of France.

TOURISM

More tourists visit France each year than any other country in the world. France's countryside offers visitors a wide range of natural landscapes, quiet centuries-old villages, castles, and other historic sites. French cities are known for their **architecture** and wide boulevards, museums, parks, gardens, and fine restaurants and shops.

Paris is one of the world's most-visited cities. The Eiffel Tower attracts about 7 million visitors each year. Its observation decks provide spectacular views of the city. Tourists come from around the world to admire the **Gothic** cathedral Notre-Dame de Paris and its 13th-century stained glass windows.

Paris is home to many museums, such as the Louvre and the Musée d'Orsay. From the Louvre, visitors can walk to the bustling Champs Elysées. Paris's widest boulevard, the Champs Elysées ends at the Arc de Triomphe, an arch built in the 1800s to honor French soldiers and military victories.

The Centre Pompidou in Paris opened in 1977. The national cultural center and museum was named after French president Georges Pompidou.

Disneyland Paris hosts about 15 million tourists a year.

The area around Paris has many popular tourist sites. They include the Disneyland Paris theme park, French painter Claude Monet's home and gardens in Giverny, and the Gothic cathedral at Chartres. The Palace of Versailles is the former home of French kings.

Approximately 11 million people visit the beautiful beaches of the Côte d'Azur each year. The tourist towns Saint-Tropez and Cannes were originally fishing villages. The most popular city to visit after Paris is Nice. The largest city in the Côte d'Azur, Nice attracts 5 million visitors each year.

Skiers, climbers, hikers, and mountain bikers flock to the French Alps. Chamonix-Mont-Blanc, a resort in the Rhône-Alpes region, was the site of the 1924 Winter Olympics. Mont Blanc is one of the most-visited hiking destinations in Europe. Wine lovers from around the world travel through France's wine regions, including Bordeaux, Burgundy, Champagne, and the Rhône and Loire Valleys.

Many people visit Mont-Saint-Michel, an island just off the coast of the Normandy region. Its historic **abbey** was built in the 11th century. A village surrounds the abbey. Mont-Saint-Michel has been declared a World Heritage Site by **UNESCO**.

Tourism BY THE NUMBERS

83 MILLION
Number of tourists who visit France each year.

1,665 Number of steps to reach the Eiffel Tower's highest observation deck.

5 Million Yearly total of visitors to Mont-Saint-Michel.

35,000 Number of works of art on display at the Louvre museum.

More than 80,000 skiers visit Chamonix-Mont-Blanc each winter.

INDUSTRY

About one-fourth of French workers are employed in manufacturing. The agri-food industry includes more than 10,000 companies with about 500,000 workers. These people turn agricultural products into food items sold in France and around the world. They include cheeses, butter, cooking oils, wine, and foie gras, which is made from goose or duck liver. The French agri-food industry is the second-largest in the world, after the United States. France is the largest producer of wine in the world.

France has two large vehicle manufacturers, Peugeot SA and Renault. Michelin produces 166 million tires a year. The manufacture and design of high-speed trains and tracks is also a large business in France. Alstom, one of France's largest employers, helps develop energy, power, and rail systems, including the high-speed train called *train à grande vitesse*, or TGV. The aerospace industry produces aircraft and missiles.

The chemical industry in France is the EU's second largest, after Germany. It employs about 180,000 people. The industry's products include **petrochemicals** and specialty chemicals used in perfume manufacturing.

4 Million
Number of cars produced each year by Peugeot SA and Renault.

18,000 Number of workers in France employed by Alstom.

#2 Ranking of France, after the United States, for number of video games produced in 2012.

About 1,000
Number of different types of cheese made in France.

Alstom manufactured France's first regional express trains in 2013. The Régiolis trains travel between Bordeaux and Langon.

GOODS AND SERVICES

About two-thirds of workers in France are employed in the service industry. People in this industry provide services rather than make goods. Service workers include government officials, doctors and nurses, teachers, lawyers, bankers, and taxi drivers. People who work for tour companies, hotels, and restaurants are also service workers.

As a member of the European Union, France can trade easily with other EU countries. There are no **tariffs** or other limits on the movement of goods and services between EU members. Eighteen EU countries, including France, share the same currency, the euro. France sends the largest quantities of its **exports** to EU members Germany, Belgium, Italy, Spain, Great Britain, and the Netherlands. Outside the EU, France has the largest volume of trade with the United States, Russia, and China.

France's central location in Western Europe makes it easy to **import** and export goods. A large network of roads and 122 airports help move products quickly. The city of Marseille has the largest port in France. About 11,000 ships stop at this gateway to the Mediterranean each year. The Chunnel, or Channel Tunnel, is the world's longest undersea tunnel. It connects France and Great Britain by three separate rail tunnels that are 31 miles (50 km) long.

Shop assistants are part of the service industry. Many of these jobs are located in Paris and other major cities.

INDIGENOUS PEOPLES

Based on stone tools found in the south of France, scientists believe people may have lived in the area 1.5 million years ago. The Dordogne region of southwest France has many **prehistoric** sites, including the Vézère Valley caves. Cave paintings and human remains believed to be possibly 35,000 years old have been discovered there. People who lived in France from around 4,000 BC left behind **megaliths** in many regions.

Celtic tribes from other areas of Europe had settled in what is now France by around 800 BC. They were known as the Gauls. In about 50 BC, the Roman general Julius Caesar and his armies conquered Gaul. The area that is now France was ruled by ancient Rome for more than 500 years. Many Roman buildings and other structures still stand today.

In about 500 AD, the Franks, a tribe from Germany, moved into the area and gained control. The region was named Francia after the Frankish people. It later became known as France.

16,000 Years Old
Age of the cave paintings at Lascaux in the Vézère Valley.

3,000 Approximate number of megaliths found in Carnac, a village in Brittany.

50,000
Weight of the Pont du Gard in tons. (45,000 tonnes)

In about 19 BC, Romans built an aqueduct, or water bridge, over the Gard River near the city of Nîmes. It is called the Pont du Gard, or "bridge over the Gard."

EARLY SETTLERS

France has had many different **dynasties**, **empires**, and rulers who each played a part in building the country. Often, changes came about as a result of war, invasion, and revolution. Many wars were fought over religious differences, to gain new territory, or to win new freedoms.

15
Age at which Clovis became king.

768 Year that Charlemagne became king of the Franks.

18 Number of children Charlemagne had.

After taking control from the Romans in the 5th century, the Franks ruled what is now France. Their first ruler, King Clovis, brought the Christian religion to the country. This was the start of the Merovingian Dynasty, which lasted 200 years.

The Carolingian Dynasty followed. Charlemagne, or Charles the Great, was a leader of this dynasty, which lasted from 751 to 987. He introduced the concept of writing down and enforcing laws. This leader also established new systems of money and lending, weights and measures, and education.

Charlemagne brought a system called feudalism to France. In feudalism, a king owns all the land and provides land to lords and barons in exchange for their loyalty. These people of noble rank or birth, in turn, give land to knights who serve them in times of war.

Under feudalism, most people were peasants. They worked the land for the nobles but owned nothing.

THE AGE OF EXPLORATION

nder Charlemagne's rule, France expanded its territory into other areas of Europe. However, the country was under constant invasion by Vikings from Northern Europe, Saracens from the Middle East, Basques from Spain, and Saxons from Germany. In exchange for peace, the Viking invaders were given a region of France. They became known as the Normans, and the region of Normandy is named for them.

William the Conqueror, a duke of Normandy, led an invasion across the English Channel and became king of England in 1066. This began many years of conflict between England and France. Struggle between the two countries over control of France led to the Hundred Years' War, which began in 1337. Eventually, the French were victorious. The war helped to unify the many different regions of France.

Exploration was important to the growth of France's wealth and power. Beginning in the 1500s, French explorers sailed to many parts of the world, and France established **colonies** in Africa, Asia, and the Caribbean. This explains why French language and culture are part of so many places around the world today. Natural resources and products such as sugar, rice, and rubber were brought to France from its colonies.

In 1429, a French peasant girl named Joan of Arc led French soldiers to victory in the Battle of Orléans during the Hundred Years' War with England.

Many French explorers sailed to North America to claim land and establish colonies. Jacques Cartier first reached the continent in 1534. The area that he claimed eventually became a part of Canada. Samuel de Champlain later established the colony of New France in today's Canadian province of Quebec. Although France lost the land to Great Britain at the end of the French and Indian War in 1763, French is still widely spoken in Quebec and other parts of Canada. France also claimed a large area of land west of the Mississippi River. It later sold this land to the United States in the Louisiana Purchase of 1803.

Within France, anger increased by the late 1700s over the fact that the king and nobles had great wealth while so many other people went hungry. This anger resulted in the French Revolution. King Louis XVI was removed from power, and in 1793, he was killed. General Napoleon Bonaparte became ruler of France in 1799 and was crowned emperor in 1804. Through his military campaigns, Napoleon conquered most of Western Europe before being finally defeated in 1815.

In 1815, Napoleon and his army were defeated by British, Dutch, Belgian, and German troops at the Battle of Waterloo, which was fought in today's Belgium.

The Age of Exploration
BY THE NUMBERS

116 Years
Actual length of the Hundred Years' War.

72 Number of years, from 1643 to 1715, Louis XIV was king, longer than any other French ruler.

40,000 Number of people who died during the French Revolution.

$15 Million Amount the United States paid to France for the Louisiana Purchase.

20 Number of days it took explorer Jacques Cartier to sail from Saint-Malo, France, to Newfoundland, Canada.

POPULATION

France, including overseas territories, has a population of almost 66 million people. That is about 266 people per square mile (103 per sq. km). The average for the United States is 89 people per square mile (34 per sq. km).

The population is not evenly spread out over the 22 regions of France. The largest region, which includes the city of Paris, is the Île-de-France. Almost one-fifth of France's population lives there.

More than three-quarters of France's population lives in **urban** areas. Paris and its suburbs are home to more than 10.6 million people. Marseille is the next largest city. Including communities around it, the city has almost 1.5 million people. Lyon has a slightly smaller population.

Between 4 million and 5 million people living in France today are **immigrants**. Some have moved to France from other EU countries, including Portugal, Spain, Italy, and Poland. Others have come from Arab countries in North Africa that are former French colonies, such as Algeria and Morocco. Some immigrants are from areas France once controlled in Asia and Central Africa.

Population growth in France has been slow in recent years. Many families do not have a large number of children.

Population BY THE NUMBERS

21 Number of countries in the world that have larger populations than France.

18.7%

Portion of France's population under the age of 15.

0.5% Yearly population growth rate in 2013.

63 Million Approximate population of mainland France and Corsica.

POLITICS AND GOVERNMENT

France is a republic. That means its citizens elect the head of state, who is the highest government official. In France, the head of state is called the president.

The current republic is France's fifth. The First Republic was established in 1792, during the French Revolution. The Second Republic lasted from 1848 to 1852. The Third Republic, which began in 1870, ended during World War II when Germany invaded France in 1940.

In 1946, a year after Germany was defeated, the Fourth Republic began. General Charles de Gaulle was elected president and established the Fifth Republic in 1958. A **constitution** outlines its laws and principles.

The president is elected for a five-year term and can serve no more than two terms. Besides the president, the French national government includes a prime minister and a legislature. The legislature, or parliament, passes new laws. It has two chambers.

The main chamber is the National Assembly, with 577 members, called deputies. The second chamber is the Senate, which has less power than the National Assembly. The prime minister, appointed by the president, is often a leader of the political party with the largest number of deputies in the National Assembly. The prime minister is the head of the **cabinet**, which is called the Council of Ministers.

17 Number of times the constitution of the Fifth Republic has been amended, or changed, since 1958.

9 Number of members in France's Constitutional Council, which can decide whether new laws agree with the constitution.

319 Number of Senate members.

2012 Year that 24th French president François Hollande took office.

The French National Assembly meets in the Bourbon Palace in Paris.

CULTURAL GROUPS

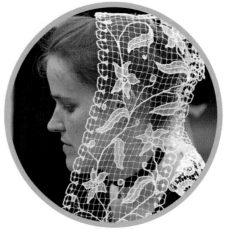

France's population includes many different cultural groups. Throughout history, distinct peoples settled in different regions of France. Today, some of these groups still live there. The Alsace-Lorraine region in eastern France has many people of German descent. Basques live in the western Pyrenees in southwest France, as well as in northern Spain. The origins of their language are unknown, and Basque is not related to any other European language. Most Catalonians are in northeastern Spain, but some live in southeastern France. Brittany, in western France, is home to the Bretons. They are descendants of the Celtic people. Their music, language, and culture are similar to those in Celtic areas such as Wales, Scotland, and Ireland.

Some people in Brittany celebrate Breton culture with parades and festivals on Bastille Day. Women wear traditional black clothes and lace headdresses.

Corsican is a traditional language still spoken by some people on the French island of Corsica today.

France's official language is French. It is spoken by almost everyone in the country. Some people speak other languages and **dialects**. German and Italian are spoken in the areas of France that border countries speaking those languages. Flemish, spoken in northern Belgium, is also common in a small section of northern France. Older regional dialects are spoken by small numbers of people. These dialects include Alsatian, Breton, Basque, Catalan, and Provençal. Recent immigrants to France speak a variety of non-European languages, such as Chinese, Turkish, and Arabic.

France is a largely Catholic country. About 1 million people in the country are Protestant. Muslims, or people who follow Islam, are a growing portion of the population in France. They make up one of the largest Muslim groups in Europe. Many are of North African descent. Jewish people have lived in France since ancient Roman times. Today, about 700,000 people in France are Jewish.

More than three-quarters of the people in France follow the Catholic faith, although many do not attend church often.

Cultural Groups BY THE NUMBERS

88% Portion of people in France who speak French as their first language.

77,000 Number of Jewish people in France who died in the **Holocaust**.

5 to 10% Portion of people in France who follow Islam.

25% Fraction of the population of Brittany that speaks Breton.

ARTS AND ENTERTAINMENT

A rt of all kinds is an important part of French culture. In 1959, the national government established the Ministry of Cultural Affairs to encourage, promote, and preserve the arts in France. That includes museums, architecture, historical monuments, libraries, and theaters.

Art in France has changed through history. Art and architecture during the **Middle Ages** and the **Renaissance** often related to religion and the Catholic Church. One of the best-known art movements is Impressionism, which developed in France in the late 1800s. French painters Claude Monet, Pierre-Auguste Renoir, and Berthe Morisot were part of this movement.

The electronic music of the French duo called Daft Punk is popular around the world.

Claude Monet painted *Garden at Sainte-Adresse* in 1867. The painting captures an impression of a moment by showing how light affects color and texture.

Traditional music is influenced by the different cultures and groups of France. Folk music from the south of France, with a Spanish or Italian sound, is influenced by Romany music. In the east, folk music sounds more German. Traditional instruments include the piano accordion and the French bagpipe, or bodega. French classical music composers include Camille Saint-Saëns, Claude Debussy, and Maurice Ravel. Among the well-known popular-music singers of the 20th and 21st centuries are Edith Piaf, Maurice Chevalier, and Charles Aznavour.

French writers have produced many influential works of literature. They include Alexandre Dumas, author of *The Three Musketeers*, and Victor Hugo, who wrote *Les Misérables*. Author Jules Verne helped shape science fiction writing with his novel *Twenty Thousand Leagues Under the Sea*.

France is often called the birthplace of film. From filmmaker George Méliès in the early 1900s to director François Truffaut in the 1950s and 1960s, French cinema has influenced moviemaking around the world. The Festival de Cannes, the largest film festival in the world, is held every spring in the south of France. French film stars Catherine Deneuve, Gérard Depardieu, and Marion Cotillard have had international success.

1895
Year French filmmakers Louis and Auguste Lumière invented the Cinématographe, a movie camera and projector.

$10 Billion Amount the French government spent on the arts in 2013.

1,200 Number of museums in France.

The Académie Royal de Danse was established in 1661 by Louis XIV. Today, it is known as the Paris Opéra Ballet.

SPORTS

Soccer, known as football, is the most popular sport in France. France's national team plays for the country in international competitions. In 1998, France won the International Federation of Association Football (FIFA) men's World Cup, beating Brazil in the final. Within France, there are several major professional leagues for men and one for women. The French Football Federation, founded in 1919, regulates professional and amateur football in the country. It establishes rules, monitors how football is taught, and organizes and develops teams. French fans watch both live and televised games.

Thierry Henry of France is the country's all-time top goal-scorer.

Tennis is another popular sport for French players and fans alike. Many children in France play tennis at school. The game of tennis may be based on a French handball game from the 12th century called *jeu de paume*, or "palm game."

Each spring, the French Open tournament, founded in 1891, takes place in Paris. The competition is the second of four international professional Grand Slam tennis championships each year. Well-known French players have included René Lacoste, Suzanne Lenglen, Yannick Noah, and Amélie Mauresmo.

Amélie Mauresmo captured the women's singles titles at the Australian Open and Wimbledon in 2006.

The Tour de France, started in 1903, is a professional bicycle race that draws competitors from around the world. Cyclists, riding throughout France, are often faced with challenging landscapes and changing weather. The demanding race lasts for three weeks. Each day is a stage in the race, and cyclists have only a few days of rest. Cyclists race in teams of nine with a single captain. In the end, the one rider with the lowest total time for all stages is named the winner.

France also hosts many motor-sports events. The 24 Hours of Le Mans, the world's oldest active sports-car race, has been held every year since 1923. France hosts a Formula One Grand Prix auto race each year. The tradition of Grand Prix racing began in France in 1906 with the French Grand Prix.

Winners of the Tour de France have come from the EU as well the United States and Australia.

Sports
BY THE NUMBERS

2,000 Miles
Approximate length of the Tour de France cycling race. (3,200 km)

1.85 MILLION
Number of professional and amateur soccer players registered with the French Football Federation in 2012.

1983

Year Yannick Noah won the men's singles title at the French Open tennis tournament.

Mapping France

We use many tools to interpret maps and to understand the locations of features such as cities, states, lakes, and rivers. The map below has many tools to help interpret information on the map of France.

Map of France

MAP LEGEND

★ Capital City
● City
▽ Body of Water
◇ River
-·-·- Country Border
▲ Mountains
◇ Longitude & Latitude
☐ France
☐ Other Countries

SCALE

N
W · E
S

0   100 kilometers

0   100 miles

Mapping Tools

- The compass rose shows north, south, east, and west. The points in between represent northeast, northwest, southeast, and southwest.
- The map scale shows that the distances on a map represent much longer distances in real life. If you measure the distance between objects on a map, you can use the map scale to calculate the actual distance in miles or kilometers between those two points.
- The lines of latitude and longitude are long lines that appear on maps. The lines of latitude run east to west and measure how far north or south of the equator a place is located. The lines of longitude run north to south and measure how far east or west of the Prime Meridian a place is located. A location on a map can be found by using the two numbers where latitude and longitude meet. This number is called a coordinate and is written using degrees and direction. For example, the city of Paris would be found at 49°N and 2°E on a map.

Map It!

Using the map and the appropriate tools, complete the activities below.

Locating with latitude and longitude

1. Which body of water is located at 45°N and 4°W?
2. Which mountain is located at 46°N and 7°E?
3. Which city is found at 43°N and 5°E?

Distances between points

4. Using the map scale and a ruler, calculate the approximate distance between Paris and Nice.
5. Using the map scale and a ruler, calculate the approximate distance between Bordeaux and Toulouse.
6. Using the map scale and a ruler, calculate the approximate length of the Seine River.

ANSWERS 1. Bay of Biscay 2. Mont Blanc 3. Marseille 4. 428 miles (689 km) 5. 130 miles (209 km) 6. 482 miles (776 km)

Quiz Time

Test your knowledge of France by answering these questions.

1 What is the capital of France?

2 What is the name of the river that runs though Paris?

3 What is the French Riviera also known as in France?

4 What is a sanglier?

5 What is the largest fruit crop grown in France?

6 About how many people visit France each year?

7 What portion of France's workforce is employed in the service industry?

8 Who was the French general and emperor who conquered most of Western Europe?

9 Who established the Fifth Republic?

10 What is the most popular sport in France?

Key Words

abbey: a church connected to other buildings where monks live

alpine: relating to high mountains

architecture: the style in which buildings are designed

cabinet: a group of officials who give advice to a government leader

colonies: areas or countries that are under the control of another country

constitution: a written document stating a country's basic principles and laws

dialects: versions of a language that are spoken or known only in certain areas or by certain groups of people

dynasties: successions of rulers from the same family

economy: the wealth and resources of a country or area

empires: groups of nations or territories headed by a single ruler

exports: goods a country sells to another country

glaciers: large slow-moving sheets of ice

Gothic: a style of architecture common in Europe from the 1100s to the 1500s

Holocaust: the mass murder of European Jews and others by the Nazis during World War II

hydropower: power produced using the energy of moving water, such as in a river

immigrants: people who move to a new country or area to live and work

import: to bring in goods from another country

massif: a large mountainous mass of elevated land

megaliths: large stones that are part of prehistoric monuments

Middle Ages: the medieval period in Europe from roughly 500 AD to the start of the Renaissance

petrochemicals: substances made by the processing or refining of petroleum or natural gas

potash: chemical compounds that contain potassium and are mostly used for fertilizers

prehistoric: referring to the period of history in the distant past before people knew how to write

Renaissance: a period in Europe from the 14th to the 17th centuries marked by great artistic achievements inspired by ancient Greece and Rome

species: groups of individuals with common characteristics

tariffs: taxes on goods brought into a country from other countries

tributary: a river that flows into another, often larger river

UNESCO: the United Nations Educational, Scientific, and Cultural Organization, whose main goals are to promote world peace and eliminate poverty through education, science, and culture

urban: relating to a city or town

Index

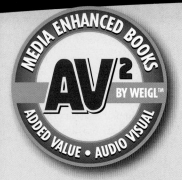

Log on to www.av2books.com

AV² by Weigl brings you media enhanced books that support active learning. Go to www.av2books.com, and enter the special code found on page 2 of this book. You will gain access to enriched and enhanced content that supplements and complements this book. Content includes video, audio, weblinks, quizzes, a slide show, and activities.

AV² Online Navigation

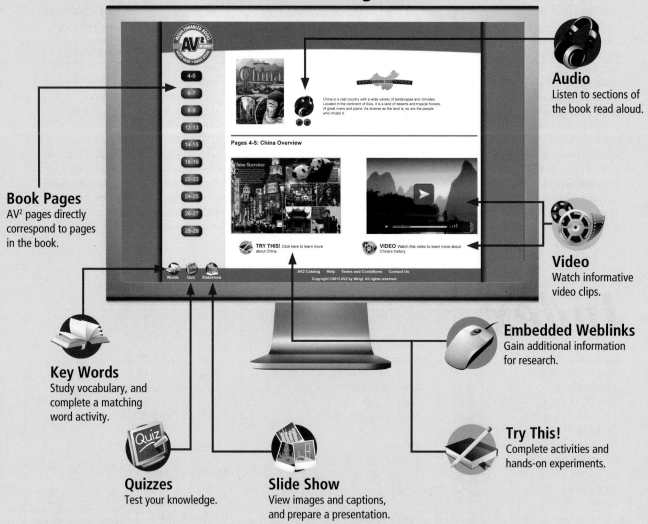

Book Pages
AV² pages directly correspond to pages in the book.

Audio
Listen to sections of the book read aloud.

Video
Watch informative video clips.

Key Words
Study vocabulary, and complete a matching word activity.

Quizzes
Test your knowledge.

Slide Show
View images and captions, and prepare a presentation.

Embedded Weblinks
Gain additional information for research.

Try This!
Complete activities and hands-on experiments.

AV² was built to bridge the gap between print and digital. We encourage you to tell us what you like and what you want to see in the future.

Sign up to be an AV² Ambassador at www.av2books.com/ambassador.

Due to the dynamic nature of the Internet, some of the URLs and activities provided as part of AV² by Weigl may have changed or ceased to exist. AV² by Weigl accepts no responsibility for any such changes. All media enhanced books are regularly monitored to update addresses and sites in a timely manner. Contact AV² by Weigl at 1-866-649-3445 or av2books@weigl.com with any questions, comments, or feedback.